7/15

W9-BWI-226

All About Sports

All About
BASEBALL

BY MATT DOEDEN

Consultant:
Craig R. Coenen, PhD
Professor of History
Mercer County Community College
West Windsor, New Jersey

CAPSTONE PRESS
a capstone imprint

A+ Books are published by Capstone Press,
1710 Roe Crest Drive, North Mankato, Minnesota 56003
www.capstonepub.com

Library of Congress Cataloging-in-Publication Data
Cataloging information on file with the Library of Congress
ISBN 978-1-4914-1993-9 (library binding)
ISBN 978-1-4914-2170-3 (eBook PDF)

Editorial Credits
Brenda Haugen, editor; Sarah Bennett, designer; Eric Gohl,
media researcher; Katy LaVigne, production specialist

Image Credits
AP Photo: Matt Slocum, 14 (left); Dreamstime: Jerry Coli, 27,
Photographerlondon, cover; Getty Images: *The Boston Globe*/
John Tlumacki, 28, MLB Photos/Drew Hallowell, 9 (left), *New
York Daily News* Archive/Charles Hoff, 26 (right); Library of
Congress: 6, 7 (all); Newscom: Cal Sport Media/Marinmedia.
Org/Juan Lainez, 4, Cal Sport Media/Peter Joneleit, 20, Everett
Collection/CSU Archives, 26 (left), UPI/Monika Graff, 29; Science
Source: Ted Kinsman, 18 (top); Shutterstock: Alison Henley,
10–11, Aspen Photo, 5, 9 (right), 14–15 (back), 16 (top), 21, 23,
24, Cheryl Ann Quigley, 25 (bottom), Danny Smythe, 19 (top),
Digital Storm, 1, Eric Broder Van Dyke, 32, Jamie Roach, 15, 16
(middle), 17 (top), 25 (top), Jeff Wilson, 30–31 (bottom), Jenny
Solomon, 2–3, kayannl, 17 (ball illustration), Paul Orr, 30–31 (top),
RTimages, 18–19 (bottom), Todd S. Holder, 22, vitamin, 12, 13, 16
(bottom), 17 (field illustration), Will Hughes, 8

Design Elements: Shutterstock

Note to Parents, Teachers, and Librarians
This All About Baseball book uses full color photographs and a
nonfiction format to introduce the concept of baseball. All About
Baseball is designed to be read aloud to a pre-reader or to be
read independently by an early reader. Photographs help listeners
and early readers understand the text and concepts discussed.
The book encourages further learning by including the following
sections: Table of Contents, Glossary, Read More, Internet Sites,
and Index. Early readers may need assistance using these features.

Printed in the United States of America in
North Mankato, Minnesota
092014   008482CGS15

TABLE OF CONTENTS

AMERICA'S PASTIME

Crack! The batter hits the ball.
An **outfielder** runs toward the fence.

He **leaps** and makes the catch!

outfielder—a fielder who stands in the outfield, far from home plate

Big hits and **great catches** make baseball exciting.

BASEBALL'S BEGINNINGS

Baseball is an American game. It grew out of older stick-and-ball games such as rounders. The first baseball rule book was written in 1845.

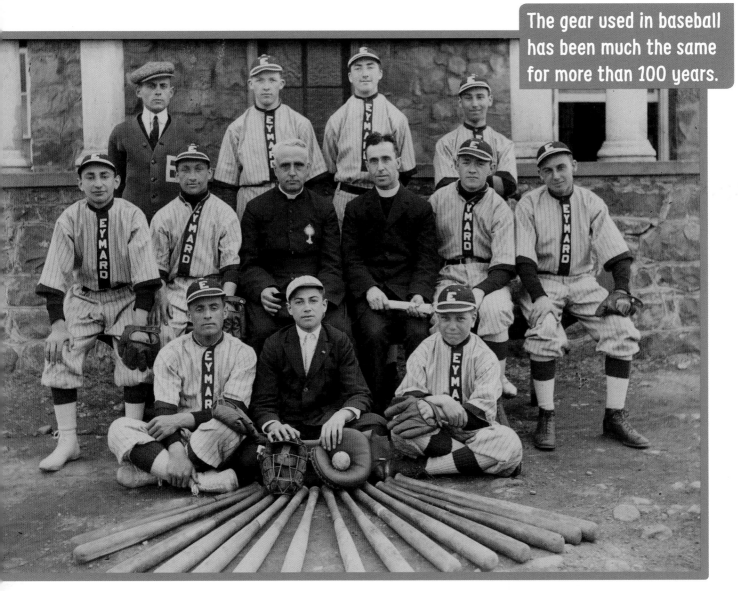

The gear used in baseball has been much the same for more than 100 years.

By 1901 the biggest pro baseball leagues were the American League and the National League. Their champions played in the first World Series in 1903.

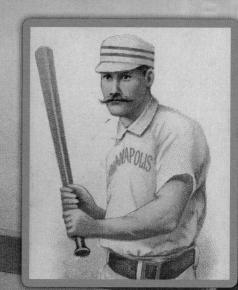

Early baseball bats came in many shapes and sizes. Some players made their own bats. Some bats were long and skinny. Others were short. Some were even flat!

THE SAME GAME

Baseball has not changed much over the years. Nine fielders wait for hits to reach them. Players on the other team take turns at bat.

The **pitcher** throws the ball toward home plate.

The batters try their best to hit the ball and score runs.

pitcher—the player who starts each play by throwing the ball toward home plate

9

BALLS AND STRIKES

Each pitch can be a ball or a strike. Balls are pitches that miss the **strike zone**. Any pitch that goes through this zone is a strike.

strike zone

A pitch is also a strike if a batter swings and misses. Three strikes and you're out!

strike zone—the area over the plate from a batter's knees to the chest

Umpires help to run a baseball game. They call balls and strikes. They also decide whether base runners are safe or out.

umpire

IN THE FIELD

Each team has nine fielders.

The **infielders** are the first baseman, second baseman, third baseman, and shortstop.

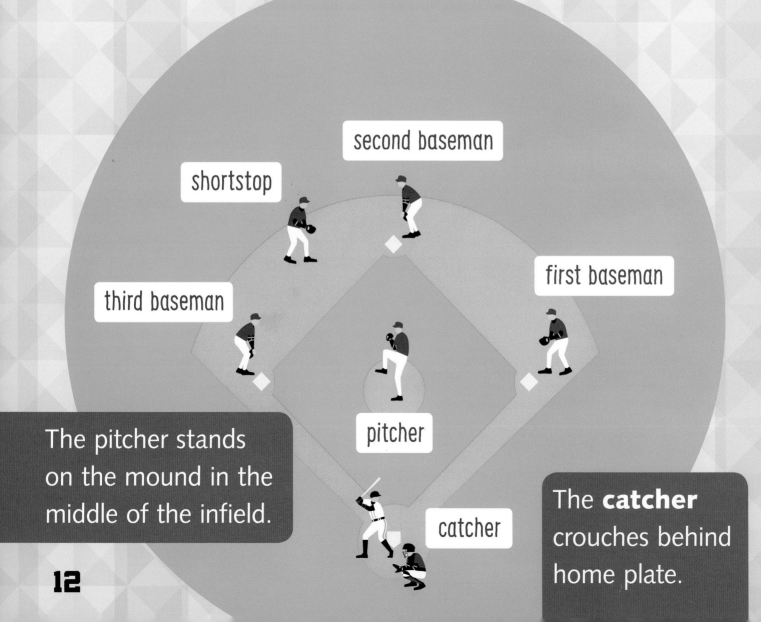

second baseman

shortstop

first baseman

third baseman

pitcher

The pitcher stands on the mound in the middle of the infield.

catcher

The **catcher** crouches behind home plate.

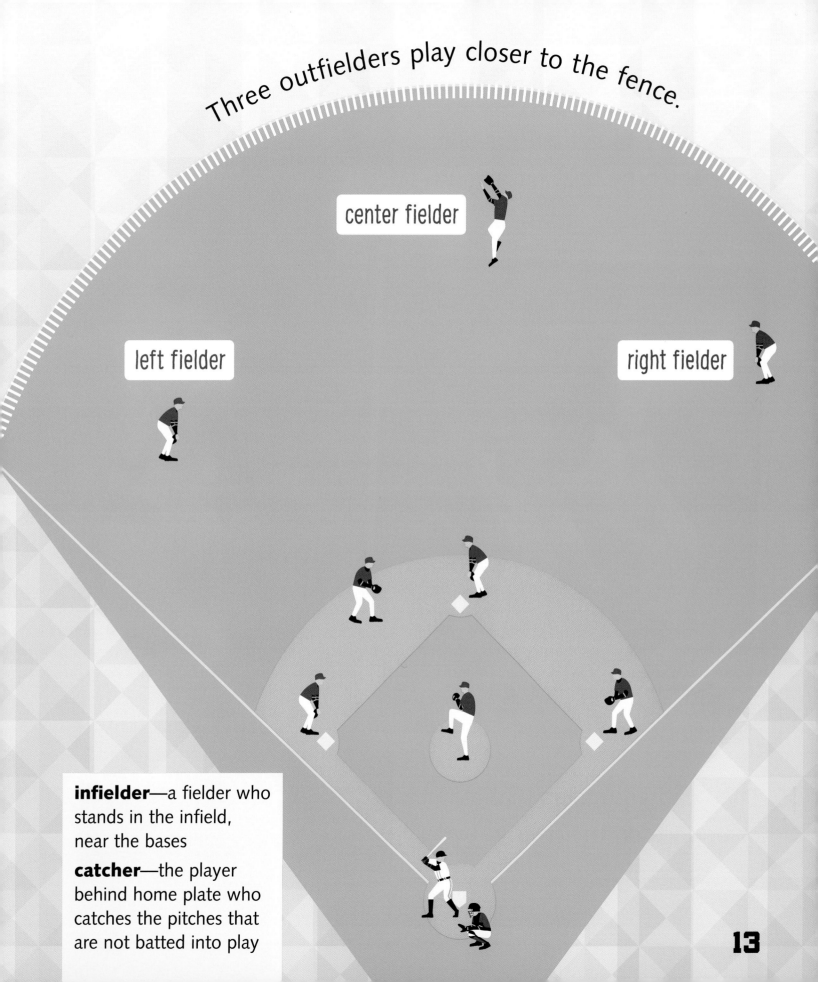

Three outfielders play closer to the fence.

center fielder

left fielder

right fielder

infielder—a fielder who stands in the infield, near the bases

catcher—the player behind home plate who catches the pitches that are not batted into play

13

YOU'RE OUT!

Fielders try to get batters out. They catch fly balls hit high in the air.

They nab grounders that roll or bounce on the field.

They quickly try to throw runners out at the bases.

If a ball beats a runner to the base, the runner is out. When a team gets three outs, its turn at bat is over. When both teams finish one turn at bat, that's an inning.

inning—a part of a baseball game in which each team gets a turn at bat

BATTER UP!

Smack! Batters reach base by hitting the ball beyond the reach of the fielders.

A base runner who crosses home plate scores a run for his or her team.
Safe at home!

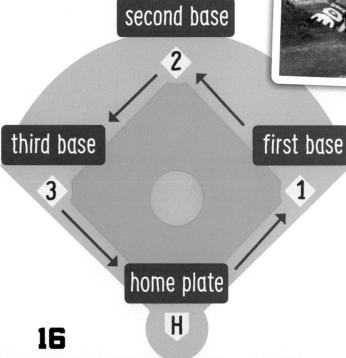

Players hit singles by reaching first base and doubles by reaching second base. A triple allows a runner to get all the way to third base!

base

The biggest hit in baseball is a **home run**. A home run is a ball that flies right over the outfield fence. **It's out of here!**

home run—the biggest hit in baseball; most home runs happen when a batter hits the ball over the outfield fence

GEARING UP

The first thing you need to play baseball is a ball.

The center of a ball is a piece of **cork.**

It is covered in rubber.

Wool and cotton string are wrapped tightly around it.

cork—the light, airy outer bark of the cork oak tree

The outside cover is made from leather.

Bright red stitches hold the cover together.

Fact

There's a lot of string in a baseball. If you stretched it out, it would be more than 1,000 feet (305 meters) long!

THE BAT

Pro players use wood bats. Most are made of ash or maple.

Hitters at lower levels may use metal bats. Metal bats are lighter than wood ones. Lighter bats let hitters swing harder.

THE LEATHER

Fielders wear leather gloves. The gloves help them snatch the ball out of the air. Fielders at various positions use gloves of different sizes and types.

A catcher's mitt has the most padding. The padding protects the catcher's hand from all the balls he or she must catch.

SAFETY

Players need safety gear to protect themselves. Baseballs can really zip around the field. Some pitchers throw the ball 100 miles (160 kilometers) per hour! Batted balls can go even faster.

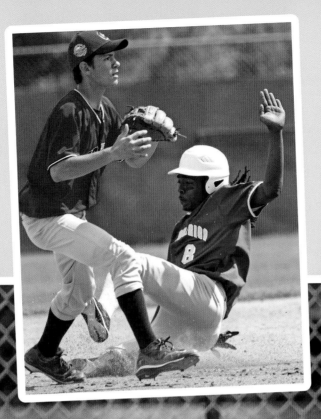

Batters and runners wear helmets to stay safe.

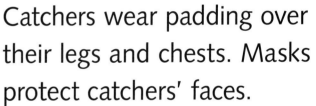

Catchers wear padding over their legs and chests. Masks protect catchers' faces.

THE BIG LEAGUES

The best players hope to play in the major leagues. Greats such as Ty Cobb, Babe Ruth, Willie Mays, and Sandy Koufax thrilled fans long ago.

Willie Mays

Sandy Koufax

New stars such as Mike Trout, Clayton Kershaw, and Miguel Cabrera excite fans today.

Miguel Cabrera

THE WORLD SERIES

The greatest thrill in baseball is a World Series title. The World Series pits the National League champs against the American League champs.

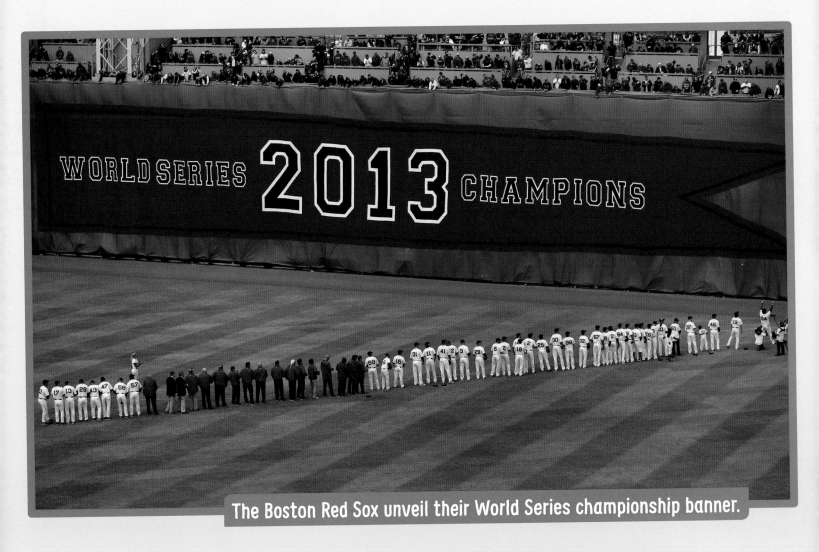

The Boston Red Sox unveil their World Series championship banner.

Many players dream of becoming World Series champions and holding up the big trophy.

Fact

The New York Yankees have won the World Series 27 times. That is the most of any team!

GLOSSARY

catcher—the player behind home plate who catches the pitches that are not batted into play

cork—the light, airy outer bark of the cork oak tree

home run—the biggest hit in baseball; most home runs happen when a batter hits the ball over the outfield fence

infielder—a fielder who stands in the infield, near the bases

inning—a part of a baseball game in which each team gets a turn at bat

outfielder—a fielder who stands in the outfield, far from home plate

pitcher—the player who starts each play by throwing the ball toward home plate

strike zone—the area over the plate from a batter's knees to the chest

READ MORE

Hurley, Michael. *Baseball.* Fantastic Sports Facts. Chicago: Capstone Raintree, 2013.

Nelson, Robin. *Baseball is Fun!* Sports Are Fun. Minneapolis: Lerner Publications Co., 2014.

Nelson, Robin. *From Wood to Baseball Bat.* Start to Finish: Sports Gear. Minneapolis: Lerner Publications Co., 2015.

INTERNET SITES

FactHound offers a safe, fun way to find Internet sites related to this book. All of the sites on FactHound have been researched by our staff.

Here's all you do:

Visit www.facthound.com

Type in this code: 9781491419939

Super-cool stuff!

Check out projects, games and lots more at
www.capstonekids.com

INDEX